LILY
AND THE
POOL

ILLUSTRATED BY
SARA STONE & ANDY YURA

Lily and the Pool
Copyright @ 2024
Sara Stone

Illustrated by Andy Yura
Layout by Fresh Design

Published in Canada

ISBN 9781738960033 softcover
ISBN 9781738960057 hardcover
ISBN 9781738960040 ebook

www.sstonebooks.com

All Rights Reserved. No part of this book can be scanned, distributed, or copied without permission. This book or any portion thereof may not be reproduced or used in any manner whatsoever without the express written permission of the publisher-except for the use of brief quotations in a book review.

For Goose -

You inspire me everyday!
I couldn't be prouder to be your mom.
Xoxo

Dear Parents, Guardians, and Educators,

From a very young age, we noticed that our child was being triggered by daily activities and having strong reactions to them. She found many everyday experiences upsetting, like washing hands, bath time, loud sounds, and unfamiliar places. For the longest time, her father and I struggled to understand what was going on and support her.

Thankfully, after we sought professional help, our frustration and confusion gave way to insight. Over the years, we saw a pediatrician, physiotherapist, neurologist, psychologist, and occupational therapist to find answers. For parents of neurodivergent (ND) children, it can be quite a journey!

As they say, knowledge is power, and with knowledge in hand, developing strategies can lead to success. I hope this book can provide awareness of Sensory Processing Disorder (SPD) through examples of what it can be like for those who live with it.

Every child is unique, and the scenarios described in this book will not reflect the experiences of every child with SPD. But I hope this book has provided a springboard for further learning and understanding.

If you or a child in your care is affected by SPD, I encourage you to seek out the support of healthcare professionals. These include occupational therapists, neuropsychologists, and pediatric psychologists.

With the right kind of support and understanding, children and adults with SPD can lead fulfilling, joyful, and successful lives.

Warmly, Sara Stone

P.S. The same Lily from this story is now a child who we cannot get out of the water! She absolutely adores swimming, especially in nature.

Once, there was a young girl named Lily
who was smart and funny, sweet and strong.
She loved dogs, frogs and warm summer days.
She also enjoyed having picnics at the beach.

While the other kids in her class were taking swimming
lessons and going to pool parties, Lily chose to stay on dry land.
That's because she wasn't very comfortable in the water.

But Lily really wanted to learn how to swim! Lily's dad told her they could go to the pool together, and he would teach her to swim.

"That would be great! Lily responded. "I can't wait to swim with you, Dad!"

"Me, too," her father added.

So, the very next day, Lily and her dad went to the pool. After they arrived and changed into bathing suits, they put their bags into lockers. Then, they headed out onto the pool deck.

"I'm so excited to begin!" Lily exclaimed.

"Let's go!" replied her dad.

Suddenly, a few loud noises startled Lily, and she almost slid into the pool without meaning to.

SPLASH, SPLOOSH, SLIP!

Lily froze. She could hear echoes of loud laughter and screaming kids . . . and she felt splashes of water from kids playing nearby . . . all while smelling the strong scent of chlorine from the pool. Worst of all, her feet felt slippery on the wet tiles.

Facing her father with fear in her eyes, Lily blurted out,

"I can't do it! I don't want to swim!" Calmly but with a worried look, her father pointed out, "But we came here to try."

"I'm too scared. I want to go home!" Tears slid down Lily's cheeks. She felt very uneasy at the pool, and negative thoughts were swirling in her brain:

It's much too **LOUD!** And it's also too **SMELLY!** Worst of all, it's so **SLIPPERY** that I might even fall down!

"Are you sure you want to leave?" her father asked.

"Yes!" cried Lily.

As her father helped her pack up to go home, Lily sadly wondered if she'd ever learn to swim.

A few weeks later, early on a summer day, Lily's father proposed that they pack up some swimming things and go out to the river.

"But I'm still too scared to swim,"
Lily confided.
"Let's just go and take a walk
by the water," her father suggested.

"Ok, let's go!" Lily agreed.

As they walked beside the riverbank,
Lily could hear sweet bird songs
and the gurgling river swishing by.
She looked up and could see the leaves
rustling high in the trees.

As they sat on a little beach, Lily rested her feet on the warm, smooth pebbles.

She smiled at the sparkling ripples in the river and enjoyed feeling the gentle sunshine on her face.

Soothing noises were all around her: CHIRP, GURGLE, RUSTLE.

"It's getting pretty hot out here," declared Lily's dad. "I'm going to go into the water for a quick dip. "Would you like to join me?" Lily felt calm by the river, and the water looked so clear. So, she answered,

"Yes, I'll try if I can go slowly."

"Of course," Lily's dad assured her. "Let's go together."

Slowly and carefully, they waded in. Soon, the cool water was up to their knees, then their hips, finally reaching their shoulders. Birds chirped, the water rushed by, and Lily felt herself floating for the first time. It was amazing!

Before Lily knew it, she was paddling her arms and kicking her legs.

"I'm swimming! I'm really swimming!" she marveled.

"What a great start!" cheered her father.

After a lot of swimming and laughing, they felt ready for a break. So, they dried off and set up a tasty riverside picnic.

I'm so proud of myself, thought Lily. **TODAY WAS SO MUCH FUN!**

She was starting to realize how much she adored swimming outdoors. The nature sounds, the gentle breezes, and the smells of summer were all so calming.

"I really don't like the pool,"
Lily said while passing the snacks
to her father.

"But you do like swimming with me
at the river, don't you?"
her father asked.

"Yes, I do like swimming
outside with you!"
Lily confirmed. "I love it!"

Lily's father thought for a moment
and then revealed,
"I think I have a great idea . . ."

He decided to make a special place for Lily and her friends to swim right in their own backyard.

And so, the rest of Lily's summer was filled with practice, laughter, and fun, as she swam and played in the pool with nature all around!

THE END

What is Sensory Processing Disorder?

Sensory processing disorder (SPD) is a condition that affects how a person's brain processes sensory information (also called stimuli). Sensory processing includes receiving, processing, and responding to sensory input from one's body and the environment. Sensory information includes what a person sees, hears, tastes, smells, or touches. It also includes how they perceive their own body positions and movements.

SPD can affect one or more of a person's senses or all of them. Having SPD often means a person is overly sensitive or under-sensitive to stimuli when most other people are not. This can lead a person with SPD to struggle with daily activities, social interactions, and emotional regulation. They can also experience problems with motor coordination, task organization, and self-regulation (which includes self-control). SPD is typically identified and treated by occupational therapists and other healthcare professionals.

For more information about SPD, please check out the links below:

https://sensoryhealth.org/basic/understanding-sensory-processing-disorder

https://childmind.org/article/sensory-processing-issues-explained/

https://thespiralfoundation.org/parent-toolkit/

Some helpful book resources are;

'Lily and the Snow'
by Sara Stone

'Raising A Sensory Smart Child'
by Lindsey Biel & Nancy Peske

'Sensational Kids: Hope and Help for Children with Sensory Processing Disorder (SPD)'
by Lucy Jane Miller

'The Goodenoughs Get in Sync: Family Members Overcome Their Special Sensory Issues'
by Carol Stock Kranowitz

'The Out-of-Sync Child, Third Edition'
by Carol Stock Kranowitz

'The Sensory-Sensitive Child'
by Karen Smith PhD & Karen Grouze PhD

Please check out your local library or online for more informative books on SPD.

About the Author

SARA STONE is an author, educator, and teacher-librarian who resides on beautiful Vancouver Island, Canada. She is an avid reader with a lifelong love of children's literature.

When she's not writing, Sara loves reading in the company of her lap dog, Cookie, chatting at book club, or drawing with her creative daughter and talented husband. She uses the art of storytelling to inspire and educate readers of all ages and backgrounds.

With pride and enthusiasm, she advocates for children with Sensory Processing Disorder (SPD) and their families, striving to raise awareness and support for their unique needs.

www.sstonebooks.com

About the Illustrator

ANDY YURA, a gifted and accomplished freelance artist, calls Indonesia home. His passion for storytelling shines through in all of his work. Possessing a remarkable attention to detail and an inexhaustible well of creativity, Andy is perfectly suited for the enchanting realm of children's book illustration.

When he's not busy sketching away, you can find Andy sharing sneak peeks of his latest projects on Instagram. Follow along at instagram.com/andyyura_/ to step into Andy's world and embark on an endless journey of wonder and delight.

www.ingramcontent.com/pod-product-compliance
Lightning Source LLC
Chambersburg PA
CBHW041704160426
43209CB00017B/1741